Missed Moments
in Legal History

Rick Chambers

Missed Moments
in Legal History

Nick Chambers QC

OBLONG

First published in 2012 by

Oblong Creative Ltd
416B Thorp Arch Estate
Wetherby
LS23 7FG

ISBN 978 0 9556576 8 9

DESIGNED AND PRODUCED BY OBLONG CREATIVE LTD, WETHERBY LS23 7FG

Foreword

Nick Chambers lists 'sketching' as his recreation in *Who's Who*, but readers of this book can readily see that that description undersells his ability.

The book contains a delightful collection of acutely observed water colours, with complementary amusing passages, depicting events from what might be called meta-history, many with a connection to the development of the law. The idea behind each picture is that what happened didn't happen, or what didn't happen did happen.

So we have a collection of clever counterfactual vignettes, all easy on the eye. We have, to mention but a few, the vilified King John and the beheaded King Charles I, followed by Captain Bligh of the *Bounty* and Whistler's mother, and then Oscar Wilde and Dr Crippen, culminating with the forthcoming Jackson reforms and ouija boards. Nick's paintings beautifully bring some very famous and (at least outside legal circles) rather more obscure figures to vivid and humorous, if imaginary, life.

I am pleased to see that two first class judges, before whom I appeared, feature in this excellent book — one of my most distinguished predecessors, Lord Denning, and also the rather more obviously intimidating Lord Diplock.

Lord Diplock hardly ever gave a dissenting opinion — his colleagues were normally too intimidated to dare to disagree with him. Lord Denning famously dissented, although, when he did so, he regarded his two colleagues as the dissenters. I imagine there will be no dissenters from my opinion of Nick's book, which is that it is a delight.

And in addition to its inherent excellent qualities it has the additional virtue of raising funds for the Barristers' Benevolent Association. The BBA does excellent work in providing relief and support for those in great need, and it is a very worthy cause.

Enjoy, and I do not know whether to hope or fear that I will find one of my own judgments featuring in future editions.

The Rt Hon Lord Neuberger,
Master of the Rolls

Acknowledgements

This book has had generous help from Lord Neuberger, Andy Allanson of Tresco Studios, Brian Hill of Wildy & Sons Ltd, Derek Brown of Oblong Creative Ltd, the ICLR — especially Kevin Laws and Rebecca Herlé, Patrick Neale of Jaffé & Neale, Chipping Norton, Diana Procter with an eagle eye, Giles Caldin with laughs and comment, Matthew Chapman of *The Snail and the Ginger Beer* where I got the idea, Dorothy Jones who bought four copies before she had seen one, the amiably dependable Peter Farr, Lady Gavron with shrewd advice, Clare Noon with enthusiastic promotion, court staff and judges in Wales and London — particularly Dame Elizabeth Gloster who took the idea a step further, Jessica Huntley of OUP who let me get on with it, my family, Voltaire, Horace Walpole, the late Brian Simpson who knew when and why Mrs Carlill died, the *Dictionary of National Biography* and artists from various times and places. I am truly grateful to them all.

Profits to the Barristers' Benevolent Association

Some history

After the Norman Conquest the nation's law came from the Crown and the Church. Rights and obligations of all sorts were set out in royal charters. The most important of these was *Magna Carta* — the Great Charter. Alongside the Crown, at home and in France, was the Church which administered its own laws. Joan of Arc was tried before the Bishop of Beauvais. Sir Thomas More, Mary Queen of Scots, Sir Walter Raleigh and King Charles I were all tried for treason by special courts usually consisting of lots of people to provide a certain *cachet*. The Salem trials were 'straight-forward' criminal trials as was that of Dick Turpin. Admiral Byng was tried by court martial and so were the mutineers from the *Bounty* who were brought back to England. At the time of Elizabeth Chudleigh the House of Lords was not only the highest court in the land but where peers were tried by their peers. It was also the place for impeachment as Warren Hastings discovered as well as for introducing Acts of Parliament which were really trials as Caroline of Brunswick did. By the time of Prince Albert's *contretemps* in 1848 the law was largely divided into the common law which was meant to be simple and general but wasn't and equity which was meant to be flexible and helpful but wasn't. The main courts were the Court of Queen's Bench and the High Court of Chancery. By the Supreme Court of Judicature Act 1873 Parliament created the High Court which wasn't supreme but did have the powers of the important old civil courts which it exercised through 'Divisions'. It also created the Court of Appeal. The Queen's Bench Division held a criminal jurisdiction which is how Dudley and Stephens came before it. And that is the way things have pretty much remained on the civil side except that usually the judges no longer have juries to deal with matters of fact and now there really is a Supreme Court.

What really happened ...

The Barons wanted it all in writing and they got *Magna Carta* — the Great Charter — in 1215 by the Thames at Runnymede. Although villeins and serfs didn't get much and King John was quite put out, it wasn't just the Barons who gained — freemen didn't do too badly and the whole idea of justice, although rather aspirational, got such a boost that whenever anyone thinks that they need a bit of a hand on the moral front they pray *Magna Carta* in aid with references to *"justice delayed is justice denied"* and similar ringing phrases.

King John and the Barons decide they
don't need anything in writing

What really happened …

At first *la pucelle*'s heavenly satnav did her rather well. It took her to Orleans in May 1429 with an army of 4,000 men where some adroit navigation ended the English siege. Next she beat up Sir John Fastolf at Patay before pushing the Dauphin off to Rheims for his coronation. But after that her guidance went on the blink. She had an iffy campaign in which she was wounded outside Paris then, on 24 May 1430, she was plucked from the saddle by a soldier in the army of England's Burgundian allies. Six months later she was handed over to the English. After rough handling and a rigged trial for heresy she was burnt in the market place at Rouen on 30 May 1431. She was nineteen years old.

Joan of Arc foretells a time when drivers of horseless waggons
will be guided by a heavenly voice

What really happened …

Although he sported a hair shirt, Sir Thomas More was witty, amusing and civilised. He educated his daughters. He kept a monkey. He was also very clever. But he loved Rome when Rome's views on Anne Boleyn were largely unprintable and his master's views on her were much the same but for different reasons. Then in 1531 Henry VIII ditched the Pope and declared himself supreme head of the church in England. On 16 May 1532 More ditched Henry and resigned as Lord Chancellor. Then Henry married Anne and invited More to her coronation but More told the bishops that going to the coronation would be the start of a slippery slope that would lead to their deflowerment but *"they shall never deffloure me"*. Be that as it may, he was tried for treason for denying the King's title under the Act of Supremacy and beheaded on 6 July 1535.

Sir Thomas More takes a fancy
to Anne Boleyn

What really happened …

Mary was unlucky with men. When less than a year old she was betrothed to the future Edward VI but the Scots decided against and in 1548, aged five, Mary went to France as the Dauphin's future bride and there she stayed until ten years later, beautiful and accomplished, she married François on 24 April 1558. On 10 July 1559 she became Queen of France and on 5 December 1560 a widow when her husband died from brain damage caused by a burst ear abscess. Mary returned to Scotland to rule but took up with Lord Darnley whose qualifications to be heir to the English throne were almost as good as her own but as a husband were disastrous. They married on 29 July 1565. Vainglorious and avid for power he joined a botched coup against the Queen that included the grisly murder of her favourite Riccio. In the troubled aftermath Mary was brought too close for comfort to the deeply unsatisfactory Earl of Bothwell who murdered Darnley on 10 February 1567 and then forced himself and marriage upon the widow. Mary's public and private life having become equally unbearable on 16 May 1568 she crossed the Solway Firth into the lukewarm embrace of her cousin Elizabeth I. A life of courtly state moved inexorably into captivity; a situation encouraged by Mary's penchant for plotting her relative's death which resulted in the execution of the Duke of Norfolk and the even more uncomfortable end of her last major admirer Thomas Babington as well as her own trial for treason and subsequent execution on 8 February 1587. Mary and Elizabeth never met.

Mary Queen of Scots entertains cousin Elizabeth
with stories of her love life

What really happened …

Tall, dashing, brave and a dab hand at poetry Sir Walter Raleigh's fatal flaw was lack of judgment. While views may differ on his sweeping Bessie Throckmorton away from her duties to the Queen, there can be no doubt about his mishandling of the succession of James I. Less than a year later, on 17 November 1603, he was tried for his life on a questionable charge of treason. His brilliant defence and meteoric rise in popular opinion brought a stay of his execution after the inevitable finding of guilt. Next came many years in the Tower of London where he wrote *The Historie of the World* and produced a variety of medicines in his laboratory. But, ever and always, gleamed the golden lure of El Dorado his ticket to freedom and wealth. Nothing daunted by returning empty handed from a previous voyage in 1595, he raised support for another go. Finally, with the King's reluctant consent and strict warning that the Spanish were off-limits, he put to sea from Plymouth on 12 June 1617. From then on it was downhill all the way — adverse winds, fever, treacherous currents in the Orinoco, bloody fighting with the Spanish, the loss of his elder son and no gold. Bereft of ships and men he returned to England and arrest. Commissioners appointed by the King investigated the failings (real and imagined) of the expedition then told him that he was to be put to death. On 28 October 1618 the Lord Chief Justice granted execution of the sentence passed fifteen years before. He was beheaded the next morning.

Sir Walter Raleigh finds El Dorado

What really happened …

King Charles's father may have been 'the wisest fool in Christendom' but he did die in his bed. As we all know his son didn't. Of course Charles believed in 'the Divine Right of Kings' which wasn't a handy line of reasoning with the likes of Oliver Cromwell but so did his wife's nephew Louis XIV and that didn't do him any harm. The trouble for Charles was that he needed savvy as well as God to keep his head on: it also pays to be loyal to those who have your best interests at heart. Unfortunately Charles was a bit short on these mundane virtues and paid the price on 30 January 1649 after trial by a court that he did not recognise (so he kept his hat on) although it seems to have recognised him.

King Charles I gets rather the better of the argument
on the Divine Right of Kings

What really happened …

Salem Town and Salem Village were a quarrelsome lot and Salem Village was a pretty dreary place — no music or dancing, no celebration of Christmas or Easter. The Devil was everywhere and witchcraft rife. The Reverend Samuel Parris stoked the tension with his crusade against "iniquitous behaviour". Then in January 1692 Betty Parris and her cousin Abigail had fits in the parsonage. They *"screamed, threw things about the room, uttered strange words, crawled under furniture and contorted themselves into peculiar positions"*. The fits spread. Accusations were made. Hysteria surged and the Witch Trials began. The first hanging was on 10 June 1692. Eighteen followed. Only at the start of 1693 did a new court and the mercy of the Governor bring acquittals and reprieves. In March it was all over.

Salem goes wild for Astrology

What really happened …

Dick Turpin was a thug from Essex. By 1738 he was the last free member of the Gregory Gang and turned his hand to horse theft in Lincolnshire. In October he was arrested under the name of Palmer for disturbing the peace and committed to the house of correction in Beverley. But the horses caught up with him and he was sent to York Castle where his true identity was discovered. They hanged him on 7 April 1739.

Black Bess was a bit late on the scene only arriving in 1800 when the story of the ride from London to York to make Dick's alibi first appeared. But real glory came in 1834 with Harrison Ainsworth's *Rookwood* and the affecting account of Bess's death after her desperate night ride.

Black Bess turns king's evidence

What really happened …

"Dans ce pays-ci, il est bon de tuer de temps en temps un amiral pour encourager les autres"

Posh, decent, cautious, self-centred Admiral Byng was not the man to send late and with limited means to stop the French capturing Port Mahon in Minorca. On the way he fought a battle that gave the unfortunate impression that his vanguard was doing all the dirty work while he was loafing in the rear. After the French departed the scene he claimed victory, left the British garrison to its fate and went back to Gibraltar. He wasn't a coward but he lacked dash and perseverance. That was pretty much what the court martial found and they put in a plea for mercy with his sentence of death. But George II was more interested in death than mercy and at noon on 14 March 1757, showing the passive fortitude that was his way, he was shot on the quarterdeck of the *Monarque*.

Admiral Byng wins a famous victory

What really happened …

Elizabeth Chudleigh was a goer. Blessed with a plump prettiness that men found very attractive she did not let illiteracy get in her way. She was born in 1720. Her father was Colonel Thomas Chudleigh who died in 1726; when mother and daughter moved to the country where Elizabeth was found at the age of fifteen by the Earl of Bath who got her a position as maid of honour to Augusta, Princess of Wales. Although the job description couldn't have been clearer, in 1744 Elizabeth secretly married Augustus Hervey, a second son who was in line to be Earl of Bristol. Whatever the original attraction of Hervey's naval uniform, the relationship did not last (although the marriage did) and Elizabeth acted as if she was free to act as she pleased which was very freely indeed including attending a masked ball in the character of Iphegenia, *"so naked that you would have taken her for Andromeda"* — which was pretty naked. In 1760 she *"appeared openly as concubine of Evelyn Pierrepoint, second Duke of Kingston"*. The relationship prospered to such an extent that in February 1769 she denied her marriage to Hervey, was declared by the court to be a spinster and married the immensely rich duke on 8 March. In 1770 he made her his immediate heir with his nephew coming next. But, after the duke died in 1773, the nephew initiated a prosecution for bigamy. Elizabeth claimed trial by her peers being by then on any view a peeress. Having been found guilty in April 1776, she left rapidly for the continent where she managed to enjoy her great wealth until she died in Paris in 1788.

Miss Chudleigh decides to stay single
and become a Vet

What really happened …

An impeachment was (and perhaps still is) a trial of someone by the House of Lords on the accusation of the House of Commons and Warren Hastings was very impeached indeed.

It was rather a shame. Hastings was a great servant of the East India Company, the Governor General of Bengal. He negotiated treaties with rulers in their own language, wrote letters in Persian, restrained corruption a bit and saved Bengal from the clutches of the fierce Mahrattas. But he was a little old fashioned in his ways and got across Philip Francis who was one of the new men sent by the British Government to modernise the set up. After years of bitter feuding, which included a duel, Hastings saw Francis off. But Francis had friends in Parliament who rallied to his cause and Hastings was summoned to give his explanation to the House. And that was where he made his big mistake.

The Commons like a manly man — respectful but engaging. What they got was affronted bureaucracy and the members would have none of it. The trial was started in 1788 with wild excitement and a battery of charges including the vexed question of how the Begums of Oudh came to lose their massive treasure.

When Hastings was acquitted seven years later the impeachment had become and remains the longest in British history.

The Lord Chancellor gets on with his paperwork after the
sudden collapse of the impeachment of Warren Hastings

What really happened …

Bligh's downfall was his tongue. No great flogger, he lashed everyone, officers and men, whom he thought incompetent with streams of invective — *"damn'd Infernal scoundrels, blackguard, liar, vile man, jesuit, thief, lubber, disgrace to the service, damn'd long pelt of a bitch"*. After the pleasant months on Tahiti it got the crew down. And then there was Fletcher Christian his chosen crewmate and nemesis on 28 April 1789. Even so, after the mutiny, he took a 23 foot long boat containing 19 men 3,500 miles to safety with the loss of only one life.

Not all the mutineers went to Pitcairn. Some lingered on Tahiti until picked up by Captain Edward Edwards who took them back to England and court martial.

After a chequered career, Bligh died in Bond Street on 7 December 1817.

Captain Bligh and Mr Fletcher Christian give the crew
of the *Bounty* their Saturday night entertainment

What really happened …

Princess Caroline was a jolly German protestant who married her first cousin George who was already married to Mrs Fitzherbert but needed money from his father George III to pay off some of his vast debts. He also needed to produce an heir. The prince was drunk at the marriage on 8 April 1795 and for most of the honeymoon. He objected when Caroline objected to his mistress Lady Jersey being made a member of her household. He wanted obedience. She wanted freedom. Even so they managed to produce Princess Charlotte Augusta in 1796. But after that Caroline went to live in Blackheath where she kept house in style and attracted unsavoury rumours. She managed to retain her position until the King's return to insanity in 1810 brought banishment from court and the loss of Charlotte. At which point Caroline went to the continent where she greatly enjoyed the company of the youthful Bartolomeo Bergami — antics which emboldened the prince to mount another formal investigation into her conduct. The evidence was in place when George III died in January 1820. The new king immediately ordered the exclusion of his queen from the customary prayers for the royal family and Caroline set forth for England arriving to general acclamation and the introduction of a bill of pains and penalties to strip her of her title and end her marriage by Act of Parliament. It was, in effect, a trial of the most lurid sort. The bill scraped through the House of Lords only to be abandoned by the prime minister. Barred from the coronation, Caroline died less than a fortnight later.

The Prince Regent and Caroline of Brunswick
snatch a cosy weekend at Brighton

What really happened …

Prince Albert and Queen Victoria made drawings and etchings of their children and their dogs. It was all very private and only rarely were they given to friends. But etching plates were sent to Mr Brown, a printer in Windsor, and one of his employees helped himself to some of the prints that were made and those prints came into the hands of Mr Strange who wanted to have an exhibition in partnership with Mr Judge who had a catalogue prepared.

When Prince Albert came to hear of the plan he took a dim view, filed a bill in October 1848 and got an injunction very soon afterwards (perhaps the speed had something to do with being who he was) to stop the publication of both catalogue and prints. Mr Judge had no difficulty with the prints side of things but said that it was his catalogue and he was free to use it as he pleased. He appealed to the Lord Chancellor who said that the judge had been right to grant the injunction because it was a breach of confidence and so was the catalogue. Although the Lord Chancellor said that this was pretty standard stuff, the general opinion is that the case marked the start of the law of privacy.

Prince Albert v Strange 41 ER 1171

Prince Albert explains to his family the moral imperative of making
his engravings freely available to the whole planet so creating
a kind of worldwide web of his images

What really happened …

When Britain ruled the waves and maiden daughters were the dutiful support of aging fathers, the Hon Charlotte Sugden occupied an exceptional place because her father was Lord St Leonards who was a clever Chancery lawyer who had initiated his daughter into his arts. This was just as well because when he died on 29 January 1875 his will could not be found although the eight codicils to it were safely in the locked box where they should have been. Luckily not only did Miss Sugden understand legal language, she also had a wholly remarkable memory and thus overcame the reservation of the trial judge that it would have been more satisfactory had the evidence of a long and complicated will been given by a professional man who had knowledge of it rather than *"the evidence of a non-professional person, above all the evidence of a lady"*. Even so being a lady counted for quite a lot because everyone was absolutely clear about her absolute integrity which was a good thing because, although she was not the main beneficiary, she did do quite nicely gaining a fair bit of property, £6,000 and the benefit of the charming provision *"that as she will be beginning housekeeping she shall have out of my farming stock two cows, to be selected by herself, out of my conservatory two dozen plants, also to be selected by herself, and two dozen bottles of my old sherry"*. The Court of Appeal agreed that oral evidence can be given of a lost will.

Sugden v Lord St Leonards (1876) 1 PD 154

The Hon Charlotte Sugden finds Lord St Leonards' will while sorting
some past issues of 'THE ILLUSTRATED LONDON NEWS'

What really happened …

Despite a limited knowledge of the female form John Ruskin knew an awful lot about art — a subject on which he was inclined to pontificate. In 1877 he decided to pontificate on a picture by James McNeill Whistler called *'Nocturne in Black and Gold: The Falling Rocket'*. Some people have been very taken by its mix of tone and colour but Ruskin was not among them. He called it *"a pot of paint [flung] in the face of the public"*. Whistler was an irascible fellow who wrote a book called *The Gentle Art of Making Enemies*. He let fire with a writ for libel and, at the trial, gave a rather impressive critique of his picture which was no doubt helped by the fact that his affecting portrait of his mother showed he could do a perfectly decent bit of realism when he wanted to. The jury gave its view of both men by awarding Whistler a farthing in damages.

Under his mother's approving gaze Mr James McNeill Whistler shows
his unreserved acceptance of Mr John Ruskin's criticism of
"Nocturn in Black and Gold: The Falling Rocket"

What really happened …

O n 5 July 1884 Dudley, Stephens, Brooks and Parker were in passage from England to Australia when the yacht that they were delivering, the *Mignonette*, foundered during a storm 1600 miles from the Cape of Good Hope and they put off in an open boat. Twenty days later, having gone seven without food and five without water, Dudley killed Parker, the cabin boy, with the agreement of Stephens.

Ruling on a special verdict of the jury at the trial of Dudley and Stephens for murder, five judges including the Lord Chief Justice, Lord Coleridge, held that to kill *in extremis* was no defence and sentenced the men to death. The Crown later commuted the penalty to one of six months imprisonment.

The Queen v Dudley and Stephens (1884) 14 QBD 273

Mr Dudley and Mr Stephens agree that
eating cabin boys is wrong

What really happened …

The Carbolic Smoke Ball Company was (unsurprisingly) a manufacturer of "Carbolic Smoke Balls". It put an advertisement in the *Pall Mall Gazette* of 13 November 1891 that was remarkably long but the important bit read, "*100l. reward will be paid by the Carbolic Smoke Ball Company to any person who contracts the increasing epidemic influenza, colds, or any disease caused by taking cold, after having used the ball three times daily for two weeks according to the printed instructions supplied with each ball. 1000l. is deposited with the Alliance Bank, Regent Street, shewing our sincerity in the matter*". Mrs Carlill bought the kit, used it as instructed, caught flu and claimed. The company refused to pay and Mrs Carlill sued. The company used every weasely way it could to try to get off the hook but the courts would have none of it. Lord Justice Bowen said that the company had made an offer "to all the world" that was subject to a condition. Mrs Carlill had accepted the offer by performing the condition and that was it. She got judgment for the money and died of flu when she was 96 years old.

Carlill v Carbolic Smoke Ball Company [1893] 1 QB 256

The Chairman of the Carbolic Smoke Ball Company
is recognised for Services to Public Health

What really happened …

It was probably not the fact that the Marquess of Queensbury was a rotten speller and lover of boxing that decided Oscar Wilde to sue him for criminal libel after he left his card at Wilde's club on 18 February 1895 bearing the words *"For Oscar Wilde posing Somdomite"*. Unfortunately, whatever the reason, the decision resulted in a knock out after two bruising rounds in Her Majesty's courts whose aftermath was a poem, *The Ballad of Reading Gaol*, whose sublime words were the unforeseen fruit of that illiterate seed.

Mr Oscar Wilde and the Marquess of Queensberry
settle things the manly way

What really happened …

Actually King Edward was desperate to get to his coronation and declared that *"he would be in Westminster Abbey with the Queen on 26 June, even if he were to drop dead during the service"* — as well he might because he had peritonitis. But at last the medics had their way. Sir Frederick Treves politely waited for the Queen to leave the room before taking off his coat, tucking up his sleeves and putting on his apron. Then, forty minutes later it was all over.

The coronation and the Spithead review had to be put off with the result that (depending on what each court thought) some contracts were ended by what had happened and some were not and the law of frustration had a feast day.

Krell v Henry [1903] 2 KB 740; *Herne Bay Steam Boat Co v Hutton* [1903] 2 KB 683; *Chandler v Webster* [1904] 1 KB 493

Nanny tells King Edward VII to cut the man flu
and get along to his coronation

What really happened …

When Dr Crippen bolted for Canada with Ethel Le Neve he chose the wrong ship. The captain of the *Montrose* was a bit of an amateur detective and even though the couple were travelling in disguise under assumed names as 'father and son', Crippen did give things away by holding Ethel's hand and regularly disappearing with her behind the lifeboats. The other mistake was to travel on a boat fitted with a Marconi wireless radio by which Captain Kendall sent the White Star offices in London the message, *"have strong suspicions that — Crippen London cellar murderer and accomplice are among Saloon passengers. Moustache taken off — growing beard. Accomplice dressed as boy. Voice manner and build undoubtedly a girl"*. On receiving this news Inspector Dew hopped on the speedy *Laurentic* which reached the St Lawrence River ahead of the *Montrose* which the inspector boarded disguised — the habit seemed to be catching — as a tug pilot. He then walked up to Crippen, shook his hand and removed his pilot's cap saying *"Good afternoon Dr Crippen, remember me? I'm Inspector Dew with Scotland Yard"*.

Crippen was convicted of his wife's murder after a five day trial at the Old Bailey and hanged on 28 November 1910. Ethel was acquitted and died in 1967.

The Captain of the *Montrose* apologises to Dr Crippen and his
young companion for the breakdown of the ship's radio

What really happened …

Mr Hicks was a well known actor and theatrical manager who got fed up with being pestered by aspiring *artistes* to give them a chance to shine, so he devised a competition that some might think rather sexist but was so popular that he decided to change its rules in a way which is not relevant to what happened next except to say that Miss Chaplin had entered the competition and was doing pretty well until Mr Hicks took the rather odd decision to send Miss Chaplin a letter on Monday, 4 January 1909 requiring her to present herself for the final in London at 4:00 pm on Wednesday, 6 January 1909. As the letter had to be sent on from her London address and she was performing in Dundee when she received it that Wednesday she had no hope of making her date.

There was no real difficulty with a finding that Mr Hicks had failed to give Miss Chaplin a reasonable chance of getting to London, the problem was to decide whether she should get anything for the breach of the contract that had been created by Mr Hicks launching the competition and Miss Chaplin taking part in it. Who could tell whether she would have won anything? There were fifty finalists and twelve prizes. The least valuable was an engagement for three years at £3 per week. The answer was to award her the value of her lost chance of winning. The jury gave her £100 and the Court of Appeal said that they were right.

Chaplin v Hicks [1911] 2 KB 786

Miss Chaplin arrives just in time
for her audition by Mr Hicks

What really happened …

D H Lawrence liked sex and Authority didn't. In fact Authority disliked it so much that books like *Lady Chatterley's Lover* had to be published abroad and then brought back to England so that they could be read by respectable ladies and oversexed children at boarding schools until the pages with the naughty bits fell out although there weren't that many as it is a bit difficult to write in an interesting way about that sort of thing over a large number of pages. Then in 1959 Parliament passed the Obscene Publications Act which was meant to put the whole subject on a sensible basis which would have been fine if everyone had agreed upon what that basis was. Penguin thought the book should be published. The Director of Public Prosecutions thought not. And the consequence was that a prosecution was brought in the Old Bailey where Authority got egg all over its face and things have never been the same.

Mr D H Lawrence thinks that he should rewrite
'Lady Chatterley's Lover' without the naughty bits

What really happened …

On Sunday, 26 August 1928 Mrs Donoghue and her friend went on a jolly to Paisley where the friend bought her a bottle of ginger beer and an ice cream at the Wellmeadow Café. We do not know the name of the friend, which is a pity because when she emptied the contents of the bottle over the ice cream in order to create a zestful iced drink for Mrs D out came (so Mrs D said) a snail in a state of decomposition and Mrs D was so overcome by shock and nausea that it was her friend who had the presence of mind to note the name of the manufacturer of the (allegedly) noxious beverage. This was important because, as the friend had bought the bottle, Mrs D had no claim in contract against the owner of the café and she had to try her hand against Mr Stevenson who had manufactured the drink. He (or rather his lawyers) said that 'snail or no snail' the action had no legal basis but the House of Lords by a three to two majority disagreed. Lord Atkin drew on the parable of the good Samaritan to show who the law considered to be the neighbour of whom in deciding whether there was a duty of care not to cause physical harm by negligence and, whatever the obvious differences between the two situations, most people think that it is a most elegantly turned piece of high minded thinking which shows just how wonderful the common law can be.

Donoghue v Stevenson [1932] AC 562

Mrs Donoghue spends a pleasantly uneventful afternoon in Paisley
consuming Ice Cream and Ginger Beer

What really happened …

Hedley Byrne were advertising agents. Easipower Ltd wanted to use their services. Hedley Byrne asked their bank, the National Provincial, to check out Easipower through its bank, Heller & Partners. There was a fair bit of coming and going but the long and the short of it was that Hedley Byrne gave Easipower £17,661 18s 6d credit on the strength of a letter dated 11 November 1958 from Heller that said, *"Respectably constituted company, considered good for its ordinary business engagement. Your figures are larger than we are accustomed to see"*. Then Easipower went bust and Hedley Byrne sued Heller for negligent misrepresentation. The trial judge and the Court of Appeal said they couldn't but the House of Lords said that, normally speaking, they could except that Heller had put at the top of their letter the words *"For your private use and without responsibility on the part of this bank or its officials"* which meant that, although Hedley Byrne had made a magnificent contribution to the advancement of the law, they did not recover a penny.

Hedley Byrne & Co Ltd v Heller & Partners Ltd [1964] AC 465

Heller & Partners tell Hedley Byrne & Co not to
touch Easipower with a barge pole

What really happened …

Although to look at him you might not have thought so, Lord Diplock was a bit of a lad. He hunted foxes on a horse called 'Circuit' so that his clerk could truthfully say, *"He's out on circuit"*, smoked like a chimney and knew the meaning of 'synallagmatic'. As with most people he saw no sense in the difference in contracts between warranties and conditions where breach of the former could never end the agreement and breach of the latter, however minor, could. So he invented the innominate term — a term of a contract that had no name and where the consequence of breach depended on the nature and effect of what had happened. It would be nice to think that from then on everyone lived happily ever after but it was not quite so easy.

Hongkong Fir Shipping Co Ltd v Kawasaki Kisen Kaisha [1962] 2 QB 26

The naming of an innominate term

What really happened …

A superbly intuitive judge who was not too choosy about his means to an end Lord Denning sometimes led the way where others followed, was sometimes plumb on and sometimes plumb off. Occasionally lyrical, always confident, he never suffered a moment's self doubt.

Leader: *Candler v Crane, Christmas & Co* [1951] 2 KB 164 (negligent misrepresentation)

Plumb on: *Central London Property Trust Ltd v High Trees House Ltd* [1947] KB 130 (estoppel)

Plumb off: *Solle v Butcher* [1950] 1 KB 671 (common mistake)

Lyrical: *Hinz v Berry* [1970] 2 QB 40 (*"It happened on April 19, 1964. It was bluebell time in Kent."*)

Lord Denning MR suffers a moment of doubt

What really happened …

Although not yet the Ouija board, pretty much everything else has been/is being tried to reduce the cost of civil litigation — fixed costs, conditional fee agreements, small claims, fast track, costs capping and now the forensic howitzer Lord Justice Jackson. Quite how the Gordian knot will respond remains to be seen.

A court takes part in a Ministry of Justice pilot project
to reduce the cost of civil litigation

For more of this and that go to
www.iclr.co.uk/nick-chambers